EDGE BOOKS

LIBRARY OF WEIRD

THE WORLD'S STRANGEST FOODS

by Alicia Z. Klepeis

CAPSTONE PRESS
a capstone imprint

Edge Books are published by Capstone Press,
1710 Roe Crest Drive, North Mankato, Minnesota 56003.
www.capstonepub.com

Library of Congress Cataloging-in-Publication Data
Klepeis, Alicia, 1971–
The world's strangest foods / by Alicia Z. Klepeis.
pages cm.—(Edge books. Library of weird)
Summary: "Describes some of the strangest, weirdest, and grossest foods from around
the world"—Provided by publisher.
Includes bibliographical references and index.
ISBN 978-1-4914-2017-1 (library binding)
ISBN 978-1-4914-2188-8 (ebook PDF)
1. Food habits—Juvenile literature. 2. Food preferences—Juvenile literature. I. Title.
GT2850.K55 2015
394.1'2—dc23

2014013956

Editorial Credits
Aaron Sautter, editor; Kyle Grenz, designer; Charmaine Whitman and Katy
LaVigne, production designers; Pam Mitsakos, media researcher; Kathy McColley,
production specialist

Photo Credits
Art Explosion Image Library: 17 (top), 26; Dreamstime: Kmitu, 21 (bottom), Ragsac19,
6, Seanjeeves, back cover, Viktorfischer, 13 (top); Getty Images: Science Source/
Daniele Pellegrini, 7, Photodisc, 29 (bottom); Landov: MOHAMED NURELDIN
ABDALLAH, 23, KIM KYUNG-HOON, 24, EPA/SHERWIN, 4–5; Shutterstock: 33333,
14, ChameleonsEye, 29 (top), Fotokon, 20, 9george, 13 (bottom), Jubal Harshaw, 8,
Humannet, 22, insima, 15, Kenishirotie, 9, Andrew Lam, cover, Malgorzata Kistryn,
28, Nancy Kennedy, 27, picturepartners, 17, Glenn R. Specht-grs photo, 16, Piotr
Wawrzyniuk, 12, zcw, 5 (inset); Wikimedia: Andrew Bogot, 25, Chris 73, 18, ComQuat,
11, Jonkerz, 21 (top), Shardan, 19, Sputnikcccp, 10

Design Elements
Shutterstock: AridOcean, KID_A (throughout)

Printed in the United States of America in Stevens Point, Wisconsin.
092014   008479WZS15

TABLE OF CONTENTS

FREAKY, FAR-OUT FOODS

Imagine the last slice of pizza you ate. The crispy crust, tangy tomato sauce, and melted cheese blended together to make a tasty dinner. Or maybe you recently enjoyed a juicy cheeseburger and some crispy fries. Now imagine eating a deep-fried tarantula. Does that sound disgusting? You may think so. But people in Cambodia find them delicious!

People around the world eat some pretty strange foods. Some people munch on bugs. Others gobble up fish-flavored ice cream. In some places people even eat food that's so stinky it has to be eaten outside.

Foods that some people think are gross may be very appealing to others. For example, you might like crispy chicken strips. But in some parts of the world people actually prefer chicken feet!

We live in a world that offers a variety of strange food options. Let's take a look at some of the bizarre foods people around the world prefer on their plates.

CHAPTER 1
BIZARRE BREAKFASTS

Do you like cereal, pancakes, or scrambled eggs for breakfast? These may be pretty common where you live. But some people like very different options to start their day. Check out these unusual breakfast foods!

MENUDO SOUP

People in Mexico sometimes enjoy menudo soup for breakfast. The chewy, rubbery stuff in the soup is tripe, or cow's stomach. Your molars will get a workout eating this breakfast. The soup's meaty broth often contains dried chili peppers and pigs' feet too.

SCRAPPLE

Some people don't like to waste anything! In parts of the eastern United States, some people use every last bit of a pig to make scrapple. Bits of scrap meat are boiled and mixed with cornmeal and spices to form a kind of meat mush. The mush is then formed into a loaf and allowed to cool. People then just cut off a few slices of scrapple and fry them up with their eggs for breakfast!

COW'S BLOOD

Feeling thirsty? The Maasai people in Kenya and Tanzania often start their day by drinking cow's blood. Sometimes they drink it plain. Other times they mix the blood with milk. This strange brew is packed with loads of nutrients. For this reason, Maasai women often drink cow's blood after giving birth.

COWS' FEET SOUP

People in the highlands of Ecuador might start their day with a hearty bowl of cows' feet soup. Some all-night restaurants in Quito, Ecuador, specialize in cows' feet soup. Peanut butter and **hominy** are often added to it to give it some texture.

hominy—*corn kernels with the hulls removed*

EMU EGGS

If you're hiking in Australia's **outback**, you could try a scrambled emu egg for breakfast. One emu egg is equal to about 10 to 12 chicken eggs, so you might need to share it with some friends. Australia's Arrernte people consider emu eggs a **delicacy**. They sometimes even eat them raw. Want to make a hard-boiled emu egg? It takes about 1 hour and 45 minutes. Not exactly a quick breakfast!

outback—*a huge area in the middle of Australia that is covered by deserts and rocks*

delicacy—*a food that is rare and considered to be especially delicious*

LAVERBREAD

Move over, chocolate chip pancakes! Why not try some tasty seaweed cakes instead? In Wales laverbread is made by cooking laver seaweed and smashing it into a paste. People then mix the paste with fine oatmeal to make laverbread cakes. The seaweed cakes are said to taste salty like the sea. They're part of a traditional Welsh breakfast.

NASI LEMAK

People throughout Southeast Asia begin the day with *nasi lemak*. This Malaysian rice dish is made of rice cooked in coconut milk. In English *nasi lemak* actually means, "rice in cream." It is often served with fried fish, nuts, cucumbers, and sometimes an egg.

KOPI LUWAK COFFEE

Drinking coffee is a morning ritual for people around the world. However, some people think *kopi luwak* coffee is special. In parts of Southeast Asia, coffee beans are first eaten and pooped out by catlike animals called civets. People pick the beans out of the civet poop, clean them up, and then grind and brew them. The animals' digestive system is said to take the bitterness out of the beans. Fans say that *kopi luwak* coffee tastes rich and slightly sweet. But this specialized coffee isn't cheap. It often sells for hundreds of dollars per pound!

CHAPTER 2

LOONY LUNCHES

Around the world people stop what they're doing and take a break for lunch. Many people may grab sandwiches, salads, or bowls of soup. But not all lunches are the same. Check out the following bizarre mid-day meals. You may lose your appetite along the way!

WITCHETTY GRUBS

Desert-dwelling **Aborigines** in Australia often eat witchetty **grubs**. These fat, white grubs are found inside the roots of trees and bushes. They are rich in protein, calcium, and iron. Sometimes people eat the nutty-tasting critters live. But most people grill the fat grubs to make the skins crispy and the insides solid.

Aborigine—*one of the native peoples of Australia*

grub—*a wormlike larva of certain beetles and other insects*

MOPANE WORMS

Many people in southern Africa think mopane worms are delicious. People often eat them as a sun-dried snack. They're said to taste like salty potato chips. The worms can also be roasted or cooked in stews. Another popular way to cook mopane worms is frying them in peanut butter sauce.

FRIED TARANTULAS

In Skuon, Cambodia, people enjoy snacking on fried tarantulas. They're actually a street food favorite. The spiders are fried with salt, sugar, and garlic. People enjoy the spiders' crispy outside and gooey middle. The spiders come from a large network of nearby spider holes. Local street merchants sell hundreds of the fried spider snacks every day.

SURSTRÖMMING

Some people in Sweden enjoy eating *surströmming* or "sour herring." Fishermen catch small Baltic herring in the spring and allow them to **ferment** in **brine** for about a month. The fish are then packed into tins and shipped to stores. The fish continue to ferment inside the tins, which begin to bulge. Fans of the sour fish eat it on flat bread with slices of boiled potato and onion. People almost always eat *surströmming* outdoors because of its foul stench!

ferment—*to undergo a chemical change*
brine—*salty water*

BALTIC HERRING

FROG PORRIDGE

Many restaurants and food stands in Singapore offer frog porridge. Frog legs are cooked in sauce and served in a clay pot with rice. People often compare the taste of frog legs to tender chicken. Dried chilies, ginger, and spring onions help give frog porridge some kick!

HEAD CHEESE

People in many places like to eat head cheese, which isn't really cheese at all. People first cook down the meat and fat from a pig's or cow's head. Sometimes they throw in the animal's feet, tongue, and heart too. The mixture is then pressed into a mold and allowed to cool into a block of meaty **gelatin**. The block is then cut into slices, which are eaten as is or in a sandwich.

gelatin—*a clear substance made from bones and animal tissue*

DUCK DELICACIES

Duck meat is a popular food for many people around the world. But some people don't let any part of a duck go to waste. In China people enjoy roasted duck hearts, duck feet in mustard sauce, and fried duck tongues. Balut is popular in the Philippines. These baby ducks are boiled in their eggshells before they hatch. People eat them up feathers and all. Want a fancy French duck dish? Try *foie gras* or "fatty liver," which is made from the livers of fattened ducks.

BALUT

CHAPTER 3

STRANGE SUPPERS

Families everywhere sit down to share evening meals. Some of these suppers look downright weird, and sometimes they're smelly. But the following foods are all loved by people somewhere on Earth.

ANIMAL HEADS

Do you mind if your food looks at you while you're eating it? People in some parts of the world consider animal heads to be a special treat. In Singapore people enjoy seasoned fish heads. Visitors to the market in Marrakesh, Morocco, can also enjoy boiled sheep's head!

QUAQ

Some people in Arctic regions eat frozen meat called quaq. Common varieties of quaq include caribou, seal, fish, and musk ox. The meat is often eaten with a hearty helping of salt. Caribou quaq is similar to very rare roast beef. And Arctic **char** quaq is just like sushi, or uncooked fish, except that it's frozen.

CARIBOU

MUSK OX

char—*a type of fish similar to salmon or trout*

FUGU

Some people in Japan enjoy *fugu*, or pufferfish. These funny-looking poisonous fish are an unusual food choice. Only certain parts of the fish can be eaten safely. *Fugu* chefs in Japan are specially trained to safely prepare the fish for eating. These cooks must also be licensed by the government. After all, killing one's customers is not in any chef's best interest.

GUINEA PIGS

Guinea pigs are very popular in Ecuador and Peru—but not as pets. People slow roast them on a barbeque **spit**. They are often served whole with spicy hot pepper sauce. Sometimes guinea pigs are cooked in stews or boiled in soup.

spit—*a long, pointed rod that holds meat over a fire for cooking*

SLÁTUR

Got a strong stomach? You'll need it to make *slátur*, a traditional dish from Iceland. Supermarkets in Iceland sell the necessary ingredients including sheep blood, livers, **suet**, and stomachs. Some *slátur* kits also include grains, salt, needles, and thread. Why would you need needles and thread? First a sheep's stomach is cut into 4 or 5 pieces. These pieces are then stuffed and sewn up at the ends to make sausages.

suet—*a hard fat from animals that is used in cooking*

SVARTSOPPA

In Sweden people often celebrate St. Martin's Day by feasting on *svartsoppa*, or "black soup." The main ingredient of this sweet-and-sour soup is goose blood. The soup also gets its color from spices and mashed fruits.

KHLII

People in Morocco enjoy camel *khlii*, which is a type of preserved meat. The camel meat is first dried for days under the hot sun. The fat that comes out coats and preserves the meat. Moroccans often add *khlii* to scrambled eggs.

HÁKARL

Did you know that sharks expel urine through their skin? That doesn't bother some people in Iceland who like *hákarl*, or rotting shark meat. To make *hákarl*, Icelanders bury shark meat in beach gravel for three months to filter out the poisons in it. But the meat still reeks of urine, ammonia, and rotten fish. People then hang up the foul-smelling meat to dry out for five more months before eating it.

KANGAROO

People in Australia like to eat kangaroo meat in many ways. Kangaroo steaks are quite popular. People enjoy several kinds of kangaroo soups and stews as well. One type includes chunks of kangaroo tail!

SCORPIONS

Most people don't eat poisonous creatures. However, many people in China eat cooked scorpions. Cooking them removes the poison from their stingers. Cooked scorpion meat is said to have a woody flavor. And some people think that scorpion soup even has healing properties.

CASU MARZU

Care for a slice of rotting cheese? Even better, how about some rotting cheese with **maggots** inside! In Sardinia some people enjoy *casu marzu*, which means "rotten cheese." This cheese is made by allowing flies to lay their eggs in it. The eggs hatch into maggots, which feed on the cheese and make it very soft. However, some people suggest wearing eye protection while eating *casu marzu*. The maggots can jump up to 6 inches (15 centimeters) high!

maggot—*the larva of certain flies*

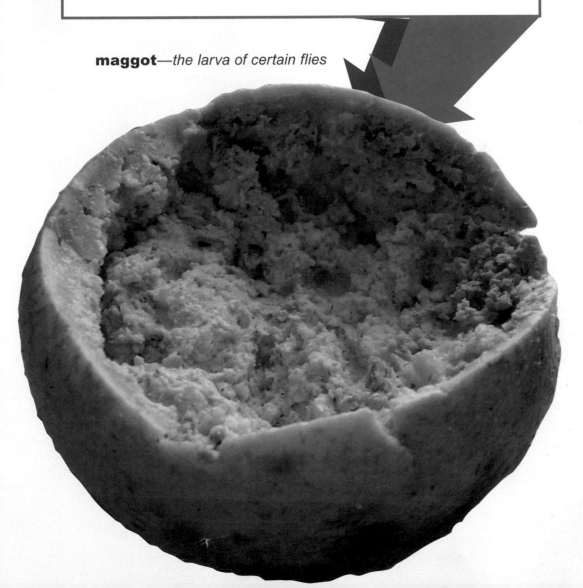

CHAPTER 4
SURPRISING SNACKS

Kids around the world often like to grab after-school snacks. People of all ages get the munchies from time to time. But you may not believe how people in some countries satisfy their snack cravings!

SNACKS ON A STICK

Looking for a crunchy snack in Beijing, China? Forget about boring old peanuts and popcorn. Street **vendors** here offer many strange snacks on a stick. You can choose from deep-fried cicadas, silkworm **pupae**, centipedes, scorpions, starfish, or even sea horses!

vendor—*a person who sells something*

pupa—*an insect at the stage of development between a larva and an adult; more than one pupa are pupae*

FLYING ANTS

In Kenya many people eat flying white ants. Kids often pick the flying ants out of the air after a rainstorm. They fill buckets with the ants and eat them straight from the pail. Kenyans also fry these ants in oil to make a crunchy snack.

HONEY ANTS

Aborigines in Australia like to snack on honey ants. They first bite down on the honey ants' abdomens, which can be as big as grapes. They then suck out the honey. People spit out the ants' bodies because they contain an acid that makes them taste bitter.

DUNG BEETLES

People around the world eat various kinds of insects. But most people think eating dung beetles is disgusting. Why? Because dung beetles feed on poop! But some people in Thailand enjoy eating these bugs. The beetles are collected from piles of water buffalo poop before being prepared for eating. Some people eat them whole, while others remove the beetles' legs and wings first. Dung beetles are said to have a crispy, nutty flavor.

STINKY TOFU

People in many parts of China love stinky **tofu**. Chefs let the tofu soak and ferment in brine for several weeks. During the fermentation process, the tofu turns black and blue and begins to stink—badly. Just how bad is the smell? People have compared it to dog poop!

tofu—*a soft, cheeselike food made from soybeans*

FRIED MILK

People in Taiwan eat fried milk for a snack. You might wonder how milk can be fried. Vendors start by making frozen cubes of condensed milk. The cubes are then dipped in batter before being deep-fried. The final product is crisp and chewy on the outside with a sweet, melted center.

CAMEL CHEESE

Natives in Sudan make cheese from camel milk. They pour the milk into a skin bag and then fasten it to a camel's saddle. The milk churns and ferments in the bag as the camel moves along. Camel cheese is soft, white, and creamy. It has a slightly acidic taste.

TREE GUM

Aboriginal kids like to chew tree resin, or gum. The edible gum of the mulga tree is a favorite. It oozes out through the tree's bark. People sometimes shape the gum into a lump on a stick and eat it like a lollipop.

CHAPTER 5
WACKY DESSERTS AND TREATS

After a good meal, many people like to top things off with a sweet treat. In some countries, people eat ice cream that comes in outrageous flavors. In other places people love really smelly fruit. You never know what people around the world will choose for dessert!

JAPAN'S WACKY CANDY

Almost everyone enjoys eating candy of some kind. But in Japan candy comes in many wacky flavors. Japanese candy fans can choose candy flavored like octopus or sweet corn with soy sauce. Many Japanese kids also like chocolate-covered dried squid. Japanese caramels come in strange flavors too, such as black sesame, tomato, grilled lamb, and even jellyfish!

CHURCHKHELA

Do you think of nuts as candy? *Churchkhela* are long strings of nuts that are repeatedly dipped in concentrated grape juice. After each dipping, the nuts are allowed to dry. Many people in Russia, Georgia, Cyprus, Turkey, and Greece enjoy this sausage-shaped candy.

AIS KACANG

In Singapore and Malaysia, *ais kacang* is a popular frozen treat. *Ais kacang* means "iced beans" in the Malay language. This colorful frozen treat includes red beans, sweet corn, and colored gelatin cubes. It is then topped with shaved ice, palm sugar syrup, and evaporated milk. Some *ais kacang* fans enjoy chopped peanuts on top.

TURKISH ICE CREAM

People in Turkey call their ice cream *dondurma*. Popular flavors include pistachio and cherry. *Dondurma* is very thick and chewy. It is often eaten with a knife and fork. The key ingredient, salep, is made from orchid roots. Salep makes *dondurma* very elastic and dense so it doesn't melt too quickly.

PUERTO RICAN ICE CREAM

Ice cream lovers in Lares, Puerto Rico, can choose from many wild flavors at the Heladaría Lares restaurant. If they're feeling fishy they can grab a cone of codfish or shrimp ice cream. If they're in the mood for vegetables they can choose carrot or sweet potato and pumpkin ice cream. They can even select rice and bean or almond cake ice cream. It's like having a full meal in one cone!

MEXICAN ICE CREAM

Oaxaca, Mexico, is famous for its huge variety of wacky frozen treats. From slushy ices to iced milk, Oaxaca has it all. Popular flavors include corn, avocado, rose, and even burnt milk. But the award for the weirdest flavor might have to go to crispy pigskin ice cream!

PHILIPPINO ICE CREAM

   In the Philippines people often like chunks of cheese in their ice cream. One popular flavor is "vanilla with cheese." If you'd like to try some very colorful ice cream, try a scoop of *ube*. This bright purple ice cream is made from a type of yam. It's not overly sweet and sometimes has coconut added to it.

DURIAN FRUIT

In Southeast Asia durian fruit is known for its strong odor. It smells so bad that it's even been banned from several hotels and public transportation. People often compare the fruit's smell to moldy cheese, dirty socks, or a city dump on a hot summer day. But in spite of its horrid stink, some people love the way durian fruit tastes. It has creamy flesh with a custardlike texture.

BUDDHA'S HAND FRUIT

Many Asian people also like Buddha's hand fruit. This strange citrus fruit resembles a hand with a bunch of fingers. Unlike lemons or oranges, there is no juicy pulp beneath the fruit's skin. To eat raw Buddha's hand, people slice the fingers lengthwise. Sometimes people use the fruit in **marmalade** or add it to stir-fry meals.

marmalade—*a kind of jam made from citrus fruits*

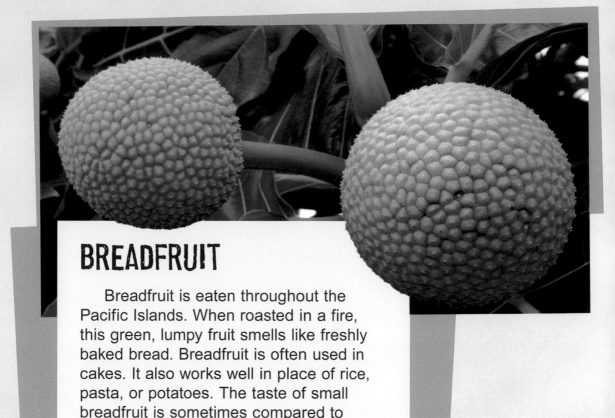

BREADFRUIT

Breadfruit is eaten throughout the Pacific Islands. When roasted in a fire, this green, lumpy fruit smells like freshly baked bread. Breadfruit is often used in cakes. It also works well in place of rice, pasta, or potatoes. The taste of small breadfruit is sometimes compared to artichoke hearts.

A WORLD OF STRANGE FOOD

From Argentina to Zimbabwe, people eat all kinds of bizarre foods. Whether foods are crunchy, slimy, hairy, or smelly—people somewhere on Earth love to eat them. You might be grossed out by some of the foods in this book. But try to keep an open mind. If you're traveling in a different country, you never know which far-out food might become your new favorite!

GLOSSARY

Aborigine (ab-uh-RIJ-uh-nee)—one of the native peoples of Australia

brine (BRINE)—salty water

char (CHAHR)—a type of fish similar to salmon or trout

delicacy (DEL-uh-kuh-see)—a food that is rare and considered to be especially delicious

ferment (fur-MENT)—to undergo a chemical change

gelatin (JEL-uh-tuhn)—a clear substance made from bones and animal tissue

grub (GRUHB)—a wormlike larva of certain beetles and other insects

hominy (HOM-uh-nee)—corn kernels with the hulls removed

maggot (MAG-uht)—the larva of certain flies

marmalade (MAR-muh-lade)—a kind of jam made from citrus fruits

outback (OUT-bak)—a huge area in the middle of Australia that is covered by deserts and rocks

pupa (PYOO-puh)—an insect at the stage of development between a larva and an adult; more than one pupa are pupae

spit (SPIT)—a long, pointed rod that holds meat over a fire for cooking

suet (SOO-it)—a hard fat from animals that is used in cooking

tofu (TOH-foo)—a soft, cheeselike food made from soybeans

vendor (VEN-dur)—a person who sells something

READ MORE

Goldish, Meish. *Spider-tizers and Other Creepy Treats*. Extreme Cuisine. New York: Bearport Pub., 2009.

Perritano, John. *The Most Disgusting Foods on the Planet*. Disgusting Stuff. Mankato, Minn.: Capstone Press, 2012.

Rosen, Michael J., and Ben Kassoy. *Strange Foods*. No Way! Minneapolis: Millbrook Press, 2014.

INTERNET SITES

FactHound offers a safe, fun way to find Internet sites related to this book. All of the sites on FactHound have been researched by our staff.

Here's all you do:

Visit *www.facthound.com*

Type in this code: 9781491420171

Check out projects, games and lots more at
www.capstonekids.com

INDEX

1337515

$20.49

J 641.59 KI